PLUG IT IN!
LEARN ABOUT ELECTRICITY

BY JULIA VOGEL

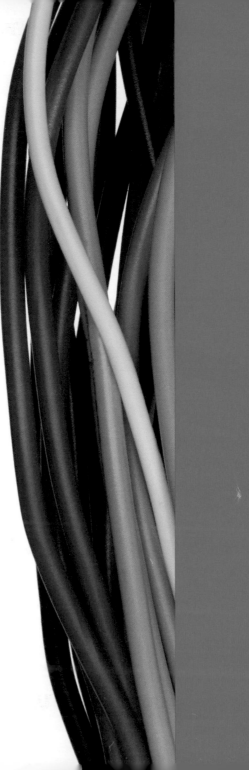

Published by The Child's World®
1980 Lookout Drive • Mankato, MN 56003-1705
800-599-READ • www.childsworld.com

ACKNOWLEDGMENTS
The Child's World®: Mary Berendes, Publishing Director
Content Consultant: Paul Ohmann, PhD, Associate Professor of Physics
    University of St. Thomas
The Design Lab: Design and production
Red Line Editorial: Editorial direction

PHOTO CREDITS: iStockphoto, cover, 1, 2, 3, 4, 6, 8, 10, 12, 14, 16, 18, 20,
22; Sean Locke/iStockphoto, 5; Sonya Etchison/Fotolia, 7; Fotolia, 9, 13; Nabil
Biyahmadine/Fotolia, 11; Dan Brandenburg/iStockphoto, 15; Vladimir Maslov/
Fotolia, 17; Jim Barber/Fotolia, 18; Catherine Yeulet/iStockphoto, 19; Dorling
Kindersley, 21; Jane Yamada, 23

LIBRARY OF CONGRESS CATALOGING-IN-PUBLICATION DATA
Vogel, Julia.
  Plug it in! Learn about electricity / by Julia Vogel ; illustrated by Jane Yamada.
    p. cm.
  ISBN 978-1-60253-511-4 (lib. bd. : alk. paper)
  1. Electricity—Juvenile literature. I. Yamada, Jane, ill. II. Title.
  QC527.2.V635 2010
  537—dc22   2010010979

Printed in the United States of America in Mankato, Minnesota.
July 2010
F11538

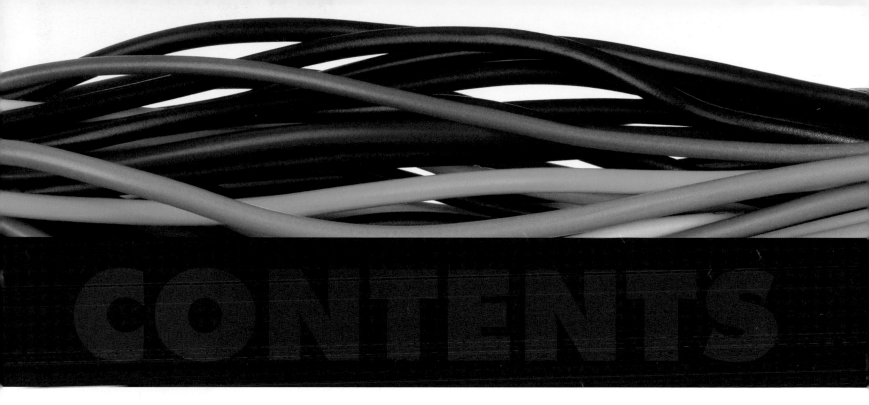

CONTENTS

Electricity Everywhere

It lights your lamps.

It spins your fan.

It bakes your cookies.

It makes your music player play.

Electricity powers our world.

Electricity lets you use a computer. ▶

Electricity is part of everything.

It is **electrons** on the move.

What are electrons?

They are bits of tiny **atoms**.

Atoms make up every object—rocks, clouds, trees, and you!

Hair, skin, bones—they're all made of atoms. But you'd need a super strong microscope to see them. ▶

Charge!

Shuffle your feet across the carpet. Then touch a doorknob. *Zap!*

Electrons from the carpet moved to your body.

Then they jumped from your finger to the metal knob. *Zing!*

That shock was **static electricity**.

Static electricity is making this girl's hair stick out. ▶

Lightning is static electricity, too.

Electrons build up in a storm cloud.

They jump from cloud to cloud
or down to the ground.

Flash! Lightning streaks through the sky.

Static electricity
in lightning
is incredibly
powerful. ▶

The power in lightning can split a tree.
The heat can burn down a house.
It can start a forest fire.

Lightning's shock can be deadly.
When you see lightning, stay inside!

Lightning cracked this tree in half. ▶

12

Go with the Flow

Scientists discovered how to make electricity another way.

Scientists put magnets inside coils of wire. Then they moved the magnets back and forth.

This excited electrons in the wires. The electrons flowed like a river. Their flow made an electric **current**.

This small motor uses magnets and wire to make electricity. ▶

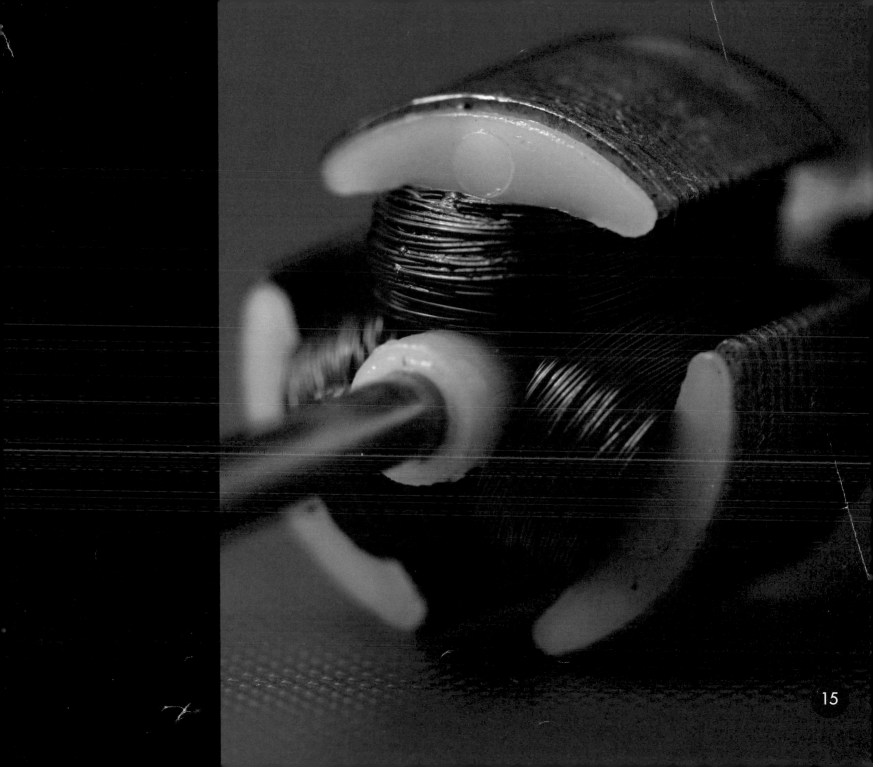

Power plants have huge machines with magnets and wires.

A power source keeps the magnets spinning.

The machines make a powerful electric current.

Water is the power source at this plant. Electricity flows into long wires carried on tall towers. ▶

The electric current flows for miles.
It travels along wires to
our towns and factories.
It goes all the way to your house.
The current flows to your TV.
Your favorite
show is on!

Electricity lets you have family movie night! ▶

Wires from the street go up into the walls. The wires connect to outlets. ◀

But you can turn off the TV
with one push of a button.

An electric current must flow in a loop,
or **circuit**.

The button can stop the flow.

Push again and close up the circuit.

Your show is back on.

This experiment shows a simple electric circuit. Electricity comes from the battery. It flows to the light and back again. ▶

Bright Idea

Imagine our world without electricity.
It's a blackout!

We all use electricity.
It's important not to waste it.
Saving electricity is a bright idea!

Unplug and Have Fun!

Electricity isn't free. So saving electricity saves your family money. Also, many power plants use coal to fuel their machines. That pollutes the air. Saving electricity can help Earth, too.

What are some fun ways to cut back on electricity? Read beside a window on a sunny day. Turn off the TV. Play a game instead.

Words to Know

atoms (AT-umz): Atoms are very small units that make up everything in the world. You would need a powerful microscope to see atoms.

circuit (SIR-kit): A circuit is a complete path through which electricity flows. Stopping and starting the flow of electricity in a circuit is what turns machines off and on.

current (KER-ent): A current is a flow of electrons. A current flows through wires, bringing electricity to our homes.

electrons (eh-LEK-tronz): Electrons are tiny bits of tiny atoms. Flowing electrons make electricity.

static electricity (STA-tik ee-lek-TRIH-sih-tee): Static electricity is electricity that happens when electrons jump from one thing to another. Lightning is a form of static electricity.